The Italian Farmers of Canastota

By Joseph T. D'Amico

Cover photo courtesy of the Canastota, NY Canal Town Museum

Table of Contents

INTRODUCTION	i
ACKNOWLEDGEMENTS	V
PREFACE	1
I: ITALIAN BACKGROUND	5
II: ITALIAN IMMIGRATION TO THE UNITED STATES	10
III: BRIEF HISTORY OF CANASTOTA	19
IV: EARLY DEVELOPMENT OF THE MUCCKLANDS	25
V: THE COMING OF THE ITALIANS TO CANASTOTA	32
VI: ITALIAN OWNERSHIP OF MUCKLAND	44
VII: THE POPULATION OF CANASTOTA	54
VIII: THE ITALIANS IN AGRICULTURE	64
FARMING METHODS	64
VEGETABLES GROWN	68
LABOR	69
COMMUNICATION AND HOUSING	70
SEASONALITY OF MUCK AGRICULTURE	72
IX: ITALIANS IN OTHER OCCUPATIONS	74
X: CONCLUSION	78
APPENDIX	81
CASE I - MIKE	81
CASE II - SALVATORE	83
CASE III - SERGIO	85
BIBLIOGRAPHY	87

INTRODUCTION

You are holding in your hands a remarkable piece of original research. My father-in-law, Joseph T. D'Amico, was an undergraduate student at Syracuse University in the late 1930's, when he set about gathering information on the Italian immigrant farmers who had settled in his Central New York hometown of Canastota. His father, Salvatore D'Amico, was one of those farmers and Joseph as a boy had pitched in on the onion farm. So when he wrote about the backbreaking, arduous nature of that work, it was from first-hand experience.

Such a work could not be written today. Most of these small farms are gone and the men who came over with their families from Sicily and other parts of Italy are long since deceased. Any of their children still living would be in their 80s or 90s and their grandchildren are from the post-World War II baby boom generation. Most of these "youngsters" would not have the faintest idea how to run an onion farm, but that was the point. For the old Italian farmers described in these pages, the onion farm was just a springboard to a better life for their descendents. As such, Joseph D'Amico's work perfectly encapsulates the American immigrant experience. The immigrant farmers worked this dark, wet land so their children could go to college, and they in turn would raise children who also went to college and then, in many instances, left for other locales.

Joseph D'Amico's first hand account, based on interviews and source-level documents, tells us how and why these men and their families came to Canastota, how they made the land work for them to build a modest prosperity for themselves and their families.

I have left Joseph D'Amico's work exactly as written in 1939, except for slight updating of the maps and tables, thanks to the blessings of desktop publishing that could not even be imagined when this work was laboriously tapped out on a manual typewriter by the author's sister-in-law. The reader may notice a certain quaintness to the writing style of this work, replete as it is with many stilted, passive voice sentences. This formality, however, conveys a respect for the subject matter that is really quite refreshing in our present era of deconstructionism, negativity and airing of personal grievances that at times passes for history.

Onion farming on the mucklands has all but disappeared. The intensive cultivation by this generation of industrious farmers wore out the land. Muck farming in Canastota was essentially a one-generation phenomenon, but that was probably how the farmers wanted it. These men – and women – worked the muck in the early decades of the 20th Century so that their children and grandchildren would never need to do so.

Much of the muck farmland described in this work is now part of the Great Swamp Conservancy, an ambitious wetlands preservation program that is returning this land to its natural, pre-agricultural state. Under the auspices of the U.S. Department of Agriculture's Natural Resources Conservation Service, this locally run initiative has set up a network of hiking trails through the area and educational programs for local school students and others interested in this impressive land restoration project. A portion of the proceeds from sales of this book will be donated to the Conservancy, to assist in continued development of this resource. I am sure the old Italian farmers would be happy to see the way their former farmlands have been recycled in such a publicly beneficial way.

The Village of Canastota, focus of this work, celebrates its bicentennial in the year 2010, so if is fitting now to finally bring into publication Joseph D'Amico's masterful study of how these hearty and dedicated individuals changed the mucklands, in the process making a down payment on their piece of the American Dream of freedom, prosperity and upward mobility.

Many people assisted me in finally publishing The Italian Farmers of Canastota. In no particular order, heartfelt thanks to: Michael Patane, Director and President of the Great Swamp Conservancy, Inc., for filling me in on the rest of the story of the mucklands, after onion farming ended; Bruce A. Wallace, cartographer at the Earth Science Information Center of the U.S. Geological Survey in Reston, Virginia, for patiently helping me search out old topographic maps of the mucklands area; Joe DiGiogio of the Canastota Canal Town Museum, Thomas R. D'Amico and Samuel J. D'Amico, for locating and providing me with the photos that illustrate this volume; and Richard Pulverenti of the Canastota Post Office for information on the painting in that post office that pays tribute to the onion farmers of old. It's entitled, "The Onion Pickers." Painted as a Depression-era public works project, it's on the wall above the main entrance, inside. If you can't get to Canastota to see the real thing, visit our website, at http://web.me.com/rabeer/The_Italian_Farmers_of_Canastota/Home_Page.html, where you will find an image of it on the home page. Those heroically posed farmers in the painting may look more Nordic than Italian and, where did those hills come from? Nonetheless, it is a most picturesque tribute to the hard working, selfless farmers described in these pages. Read on.

Richard C. Beer
March 2010

ACKNOWLEDGEMENTS

The writer wishes to extend his appreciation to all who helped to make this thesis possible, particularly to all those Italian-Amer1cans, too numerous to mention, who cooperated so willingly while he was investigating life histories and classifying the foreign-born Italians. He is also obligated to John Wilson and the others who supplied some essential information for the section on the development of the muckland. To Dr. Frank Ross of the Sociology Department, whose interest, suggestions, and supervision were always a source of aid and encouragement, the writer is especially grateful. He also wishes to thank his sister-in-law, Mrs. V. James (Susan Mangione) D'Amico for her kindness in typing the original draft as well as the present manuscript.

Joseph T. D'Amico

May 1939

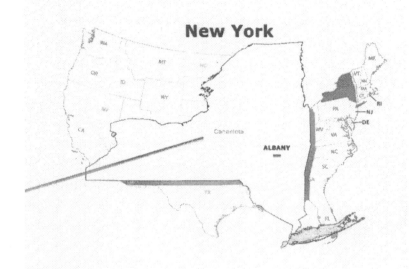

PREFACE

Photo Courtesy of Canastota, New York, Canal Town Museum

The foreign-born Italians in the United States, as a whole, are industrial workers. Ever since their immigration to this country they have, in the main, looked to the factories, the railroads, the mines, and to construction work for their means of subsistence. When one considers the fact that the great majority or these Italians come from agricultural districts of Italy, this phenomenon is not only interesting but also somewhat surprising. But, if one considers the circumstances that these immigrants faced In America, it is not difficult to understand why they are mainly industrial workers.

While it is true that most of the Italians in America have forsaken their former occupation and turned to other means of employment, still a fairly sizeable number hare entered agriculture.[1] In this latter category the Italians of Canastota, New York must be placed. Although all of the Italian foreign-born of this town are not actively engaged in agriculture, actually, the majority are not only thus employed, but almost all of them have at some time or other been connected with the onion-growing business.

This thesis, among other things, is an attempt to study certain aspects of the Italian foreign-born of Canastota, the greater emphasis being placed on the Italians in agriculture (onion-growers). This study, aside from personal interest, was chosen because to the writer's way of thinking, the Italian muck farmers of this community possess a very interesting uniqueness. This uniqueness seems to take the form of a carry-over from the "Old Country." Before coming to this country, these same Italians were mostly participants in an agricultural system in which the fields of labor were at a considerable distance from the place of abode. That is, the Italians usually lived in villages, and every morning and evening they walked or rode to and from the fields of work.[2] Among the onion growers of Canastota, a similar situation exists. These growers, for the most part, have permanent residence in the village but their fields of labor (the mucklands) lie north of the village at distances varying from two to seven miles. During the work seasons (with the exception of those Italians that move to the muck farms for the summer) these immigrants and their families commute daily to work. The main difference, probably, being that at the present time, these Italian-Americans have substituted the American motor vehicle for the donkey and the mule of Italy.

An attempt bas been made, in a general way, to follow these Italians from the time to their departure to 1930, and in some aspects to the present time. But the writer's interest has not been so much with individual behavior as it has with group phenomena. At the same time, an attempt has been made to show the resources, the facilities, and the opportunities that the village and its vicinity offered the Italians. With this in mind a brief history of Canastota, as well as the early development of the muckland was written.

In this study with one exception, only the foreign-born Italians having residence in the village itself were considered. In Chapter VI, because it was undesirable to do otherwise, those Italians who had permanent residence on the muck farms were included. In regards to the land, only the section known as the Canastota muck area was taken into consideration.

In the main, the survey was conducted from the historical approach, but in order to enable the writer to secure and present certain pertinent information other methods also were applied. In obtaining the material for Chapter V and part of Chapter IV, the personal interview method was used. In Chapter VI and in a number of other instances, the statistical approach was required since the procedure and sources of information are usually specified in the text of this thesis, it is not necessary to make further explanation concerning them.

The writer regrets that time did not enable him to make a comparison of this community with one or more of the several similar communities In New York State. A comparison might have been made with the smaller onion growing Italian group at Montezuma, New York, at Elba, New York, or at several others.

I: ITALIAN BACKGROUND

Photo of Mt. Etna, Italy, from:
http://upload.wikimedia.org/wikipedia/commons/5/5a/Sommer%2C_Giorgio_%28183-1914%29___Catania_e_I%27Etna.jpg

In studying immigrant groups or immigrant communities in America, it is usually desirable that an attempt be made to study the background of the people that make up these groups or communities in their original setting. Seeing the situation and conditions that these people faced in their mother country, an insight may be gained as to why they left their homeland for our shores. And also a better understanding may be had of these people in their new environment. So, with this in mind, the conditions in Italy before and during the great emigration movement will be surveyed.

In any study of Italy it should always be kept in mind that though the territory comprising Italy has been a part of the civilized world since the dawn of history, politically the Italy of today is among the newer nations of the world. For centuries this country was divided into many parts, each part being under independent rulers or under foreign domination. Through the efforts of Mazzini, Cavour, King V. Emmanuel, and Garibaldi the unification of Italy began in 1859 and it was not accomplished until 1871.

Italy, during the latter part of the Nineteenth Century and first decade of the 20th, was more densely populated than any other European nation except Belgium, the Netherlands, and England. What is more, the population increased steadily in spite of the high emigration rate. The birthrate was high and there was an excess of births over deaths. Italy's resources were not sufficient, or they were not sufficiently developed, to afford means for adequate support of its large and growing population.[1]

Many people have been under the false impression that Italy was a rich country. One poem concerning Italy runs in this fashion: *Ricca, ma ricca assai* (Rich, very rich). In reality, Italy, in comparison with most other

European countries was poor in most of the essentials that form the material prosperity of a nation. Also, the geographical distribution of wealth in Italy was unequal---the southern *compartimenti* (provinces) being much poorer than those of the North. In some sections of the North there was considerable industrial activity and agricultural conditions were good, but in the South there had been comparatively little industrial progress and agricultural resources in many sections were poor or poorly developed. Thus, economic conditions in the Southern provinces are generally much worse than in the North.

In 1901, 37.8 per cent[2] of the total population of Italy was engaged in agriculture, forestry or cattle raising. The Northern provinces, generally speaking, were more fertile and methods used were more progressive, but on the whole, the agricultural development was poor. Returns on capital invested were small, and wages paid to farm laborers were always low. In Southern Italy and Sicily crude implements were used and primitive means of cultivation still prevailed. Even under the most favorable conditions little more than the tenant farmer or small land-holder could make a bare living, and his lot was especially difficult when a pest destroyed his olives.

In Southern Italy and Sicily every available bit of land was utilized, and though the work was done in a crude way the land was carefully cultivated. In some provinces all the work was done by hand implements. The grain was reaped by sickle, and there was no modern farming machinery of any character. In Calabria a few more plows were seen than in Sicily, but practically the same methods were found.

Wages for agricultural laborers were low in every section of Italy, but they varied widely. In some districts of Sicily and Calabria, farm hands received from 14 to 20 cents a day. But the usual wage per day paid to agricultural labor was from 2 to 2 ½ lires (40 to 50 cents)[3], although in addition to money wages paid to these laborers, some allowance for food and drink or produce was usually made.

In looking into the housing conditions of the peasants it is seen that they usually lived in huts, which were mostly low, one-roomed hovels, often with no opening besides the door. The floor was of earth or possibly stone, the furniture was usually one or two beds, a bench and perhaps a chair.

The peculiar location of most villages in Italy was responsible for another hardship to the peasants. The towns were usually located on hills or on mountainsides, and always at a considerable distance from the fields where most of the peasants worked. The laborers often had to walk 4 or 5 miles daily to their work.

Living conditions were generally better among industrial workers than among the lower-paid agricultural laborers, but the range of wages paid was sufficient to show that the standard of living was low compared with the standard usually found in American communities. The poor in Italy lived miserably. Few of the conveniences of life were within the people's means, the bare necessities had to suffice, and the quality of what they could get was usually of the poorest.[4]

Taxation, during that period, was one of the greatest burdens of the common people of Italy, and especially of the Southern Italians, and the Sicilians. The great-landed estates of the South were often exempt from taxation, but the small-landholders were taxed heavily.

Malaria, in a violent form, was a scourge of Southern Italy. The disease bred in swamps and stagnant pools, causing the peasant to live miles away from his land. This condition not only caused the farmer to consume considerable time in coming and going from his work, but in his absence field robbers took toll of his harvest. Another hindrance to the peace of mind of the peasants was the frequency of earthquakes, which not only were destructive of capital, but also had a terrifying effect on the mind.

II: ITALIAN IMMIGRATION TO THE UNITED STATES

Immigrants Landing at Ellis Island, circa 1900

Photo from: http://www.nyc-architecture.com/LM/LM-Ellis-immigrants.jpg

Ethnically speaking, there are two groups of Italians, the North and the South. The North Italian is Teutonic in blood and appearance and belongs to the Alpine division of the white race. He comes from the departments of Piedmont, Lombardy and Venetia--the most industrialized and urbanized sections of Italy, where the standard of living was higher and illiteracy less common. The South Italians, who descend with less mixture from the ancient inhabitants of Italy, descends from the Mediterranean branch of the white race. He tended to be an illiterate peasant from some great landed estate, with wages less than one-third of his Northern compatriots. The North Italians, being more progressive, were the first to emigrate, going primarily to neighboring European countries and South America, while the South Italians have immigrated chiefly to the United States.[1]

There is a notable peculiarity in the flow of Italian immigration to this country. From the earliest days of colonization of America up to 1850, the influx from Italy was barely a trickle. The movement had no marks whatsoever of a mass movement, and we can safely put the figure of Italians in the United States, at this time, at less than 4,500; to these in the 1850-60 decade we can add 9,231 more,[2] the merest ripple compared with the mighty wave then sweeping in from Eastern Europe. From 1860 to 1870 there was a slight increase in the number admitted, the amount being 11,725.[3] In the 1870-80 decade an appreciable increase appears, with 55.757 being admitted, but still this was comparatively inconsiderable compared with what was to follow.

Before 1860, the immigration appears to have been of persons who desired permanent settlement; this is partially explained by the difficulties of transportation. The arrivals were chiefly from Northern Italy. At the same time, it was an immigration of individuals and families. Between 1860 and 1880, the immigration assumed a much more definite character than before. Where previously there had been individuals, there now were types and classes. During this period the contingent from South Italy swelled to a substantial proportion. After 1870 it was seen that, following a short stay, many repacked their bags and returned home.

By 1880, the formative years of Italian immigration may be said to have been completed. Its main characteristics were now apparent. It was mostly from Southern Italy, was increasingly disposed after a time to return to Italy, and had taken up a wide range of vocations in the United States. Another fact noted, is that two out of every three arrivals from Italy were men. And above all it was a mass movement.[4]

In the 1880-1890 decade there was a great increase in the flow, for 307,309[5] entered the United States, but many of these returned to Italy, thus the increase of Italians in America was not as large as it might have been. In the following period, the flow was becoming larger and larger, and more than 651,893[6] entered, so that by 1900 (keeping in mind the fact that many returned) the approximate number of Italians in America may be placed at about 484,027.[7]

The great bulk or Italian immigrants have been admitted since 1900. In the first decade of the Twentieth Century the peak was reached when 2,047,877[8] entered the United States. But so many returned that the enumeration of 1910 found about 1,343,125[9] Italians in the United States, and together with their American-born children they numbered, at that time, about 2,098,360.[10]

In the World War decade, 1910-1920, the amount of Italians entering the United States, though smaller than the amount of the previous decade, was still great, numbering about 1,109,524.[11] Due to the disapproval of emigration by the Italian government, and the imposition of certain immigration laws by the United States, immigrations fell to about 455,315[12] in the 1920-30 span.

In the early days of Italian immigration, the west coast attracted a relatively, large proportion; as late as 1890 Italians were more numerous in the Pacific States than in New England. But since then the majority have settled in New England, and the Middle Atlantic states of New York, New Jersey and Pennsylvania.

Table 2.1 Italians Admitted to the United States by Decades, 1820-1930[13]

Decade	Immigrants
1821-1830	439
1831-1840	2,253
1841-1850	1,870
1851-1860	9,231
1861-1870	11,725
1871-1880	55,757
1881-1890	307,309
1891-1900	651,893
1901-1910	2,045,877
1911-1920	1,109,524
1921-1930	455,315
TOTAL	4,651,193

Table 2.2 Foreign Born Italians in the United States, 1850-1930[14]

Decade	Number	Foreign Born
1850-1859	3,679	0.20%
1860-1869	11,667	0.30%
1870-1879	17,157	0.30%
1880-1889	44,230	0.70%
1890-1899	182,580	2.00%
1900-1909	484,027	4.70%
1910-1919	1,343,125	9.00%
1920-1929	1,610,113	11.60%
1930-1939	1,790,429	12.60%

Table 2.3 Total Foreign Born Italians in 1930 By Geographic Division[15]

Region	Number
New England	253,098
Middle Atlantic	1,046,159
East-North Central	244,504
West-North Central	31,653
South Atlantic	39,512
East-South Central	7,288
West-South Central	22,185
Mountain	23,774
Pacific	122,251
TOTAL	1,790,424

Table 2.3.1 Middle Atlantic Sub-totals by State

State	Number
New York	629,322
Pennsylvania	225,979
New Jersey	190,858

During the whole period of 1820 to 1930, Italians rank as the second largest contributors to our population through immigration.

By 1910, four-fifths of all the Italians in America were classed by the census as urban, a proportion that was immensely high, especially when you consider the fact that most of these immigrants came from agricultural districts. The greatest concentration was in New York City, where there were more Italians than in any Italian city except Naples, (340,770). In New Orleans at this time, the Italians exceeded all other foreign groups. Many Italians also settled in the other large cities of the country: Philadelphia, Chicago, Boston, Newark, San Francisco, Pittsburgh, Jersey City, Buffalo, etc.

This huge concentration of Italians in the cities of America, is partially explained by the fact that when the Italian immigrant arrived in America, be usually found himself practically penniless, and dearly in need of a job. Opportunities for finding jobs and earning quick money were much better in the cities than elsewhere -- thus most of them settled there.

Table 2.4 Percent Distribution of the Foreign-Born from Italy by Division -- 1870-1930[16]

	Year						
Region	1870	1880	1890	1900	1910	1920	1930
New England	4.1	7.8	9.2	12.7	13.4	14.8	14.1
Middle Atlantic	27	44	55.8	60.1	58.4	57.5	58.4
East-North Central	9.5	8.7	9.1	9.2	10.9	12.6	13.7
West-North Central	6.6	3.7	2.9	2.2	2.8	2.1	1.8
South Atlantic	4.6	3.1	2.7	2.2	2.9	2.5	2.2
West-South Central	12.3	7.2	5.5	4.7	2.4	1.7	1.2
Mountain	3.2	5.3	4.1	3	2.6	1.7	1.3
Pacific	27.5	17.6	9.6	5.4	6.1	6.5	6.8

III: BRIEF HISTORY OF CANASTOTA[1]

Photo Postcard courtesy of Thomas R. D'Amico

In the first decade of the Nineteenth Century the site of Canastota was far from being an ideal region on which to build a village. It was mainly a low, swampy forest with only a small clearing. It was part of the Canastota tract from which it was reserved when the sale of that tract was made by the Oneidas to the State.

Captain Reuben Perkins obtained the land on which the village now stands, and he secured a state patent for it in 1810.[2] Subsequently, Perkins sold parts of his purchase to other individuals who came there to live, until, finally the whole purchase had been divided into village lots and sold.

The first great impetus to the growth of the village was the building of the Erie Canal, which was completed in 1825.

By 1831 the population of the village had grown to about 406[3] and the mercantile business of the Village had increased along with the population. Encouraged by the growth and prospect of the village, the inhabitants took steps in these early years to secure an act of incorporation. This was done by a special charter on April 28, 1835.

In 1839, a railroad connecting Syracuse and Utica was built and fortunately it traversed the heart of the village, ushering in a new area of prosperity by leading to the development of important industries. This undoubtedly was the second major step in the development of Canastota.

In 1840, the population of the Village was approximated at 800,[4] more than doubling during the previous decade. By 1850, according to the Seventh Census of the United States, the number of Canastotans was placed at 1,000.

Henceforth, the village grew rapidly, particularly as a mercantile center and in industry. Stores sprang up, mills of different sorts went into business, and many other small businesses began to obtain firm footholds. Salt had been discovered 1n the vicinity of the village, and in several instances projects were attempted for its exploitation.

The village received its first setback in 1873, when

a devastating fire swept a part of the town. But with renewed courage and vigor Canastotans set about to rebuild it in a more substantial manner and better style than before. After this, more industries sprang up. In 1876 a lumber company formed; and in 1874, the Canastota Knife Company--soon to be employing close to 100 hands--started to manufacture its products.

By 1880, the population had increased to 1,569.[5] During this decade a canning concern was started. This was the beginning of one of Canastota's most reliable and thriving industries for the future. In 1882 a large plant for wheel rakes began to do business. In 1884, as a means of taking advantage of the excellent sand of Oneida Lake, a glass manufacturing company was founded. The Oneida Lake sand was reputed to be as fine a material for glass making as could be found in the country at that time. In 1886, Cady's Machine Shop was organized, and in 1888, a large concern, the Smith and Ellis Company for the manufacture of hall racks, etc., was opened.

By 1890 the population of the Canastota had climbed to 2,774.[6] In 1892 the Lee Chair Company was moved to Canastota. In 1899 the Watson Wagon Company was founded and this presently became the village's leading and largest manufacturing organization--employing hundreds of laborers. For more than a decade previous to this, Mr. Watson had made Watson dumping wagons, privately.

Thus, by the end of the century Canastota is seen as a prosperous industrial town, possessing many industries both large and small, with railroads and a canal as added impetus for business. Its banks, stores, manufacturing plants and churches were used not only by its immediate inhabitants but the town was used as a community center by many of the smaller localities in its vicinity. It now possessed two newspapers, fine schools, a fire department, a police force, as well as many of the other essentials of a town. Its population in 1900 was 3.030.[7]

The railroads--New York Central, Hudson River R.R., the West Shore Line, and the Lehigh Valley, which ran through the heart of the village offered, at this time, one of the greatest means of subsistence for a great number of Canastotans.

In view of the fact that the village was located strategically between Syracuse and Utica, it was being used more and more as a center for construction crews.

Because of the canal, railroads and turnpikes, which either ran through the village itself or very close to it, Canastota could at this time be said to be in contact with the whole United States, and possibly the major portion or the World. This fact, when considering what was about to happen, is an important point.

Attracted by all this, and later by the fertile muck lands that lay to the north of the village, many Italian immigrants began to settle in the village. In 1900 the number of these immigrants was relatively small, but by 1910 when the total population of the village was 3,247,[8] the proportion had grown immensely and the village contained 465[9] foreign born whites. In 1920 the number of Canastotans was 3,995,[10] and the amount of immigrants in the village now had increased to 610.[11]

Table 3.1 Population of Canastota 1850-1930[12]

Year	Total	Foreign Born Whites
1850	1,000	n/a
1860	n/a	n/a
1870	1,492	175
1880	1,569	n/a
1890	2,774	308
1900	3,030	280
1910	3,247	465
1920	3,995	609
1930	4,235	658

During the World War decade, the Watson Wagon Company reached its highest peak, when considering the number of men employed. In 1915, it had begun to manufacture Watson trucks, and during the war it sold many of its products to the United States army. Also thousands of Canastota Wagons were shipped directly to France.[13]

During the twenties, one new manufacturing plant was formed, but the tendency as a whole, during this period, was toward a sharp decrease in industry. Two of the largest plants actually closed and the majority of the remainder employed fewer men.

In 1930, the population by the Fifteenth Census of the United States was placed at 4,235, the number of foreign-born being 658. Most of these were Italians.

Thus, we find that the growth of Canastota can be traced parallel to the utilization of the natural resources that the Village had near at hand and at its disposal. Lumber, sand from Oneida Lake, salt and other resources were used to their best advantage. But slowly because of new inventions and improvements, either the article made or the process used in making the article became out-or-date; wheel brakes, dump wagons, etc., all lost their demand in the rapid advancement or American civilization. Many of the industries began to lose their trade, and finally were forced out of business. Then it was that more and more of the people of Canastota began to turn to the utilization of their greatest natural resource - the mucklands.

IV: EARLY DEVELOPMENT OF THE MUCKCKLANDS[1]

Photo Courtesy of the Canastota, New York, Canal Town Museum

North of the Village of Canastota and edging toward the northwest, there existed during the eighteenth century a level, miry, muck swamp. This black soil swamp, lying approximately three miles from the village and six from Oneida Lake, which is due north, was covered, as most swamps are, with abundant vegetation. Trees, brush, and many other forms of plant life, small and large were everywhere in evidence. Travel through this wilderness had always been most difficult and the Oneida Indians, who had inhabited this part of the state, never had more than a few trails traversing it. The first modern means of transportation through the swamp took place in 1811,[2] when a road connecting Canastota and the lake was constructed.

The realization that this swampland could be of use materially to man occurred at sometime during the first half of the eighteenth century. During this period, the state parceled out most of the land to individuals at a very low price. But, as one may well see, these individuals who had the foresight to invest in this swampland, could do very little with it until definite steps were taken for reclamation. Drainage was the first problem and it was the most important one.

The first step toward reclamation occurred about 1850, when the state undertook to construct an artificial ditch.[3] This ditch called the Douglas Ditch was out through the lands between Oneida Lake and the swamp. This proved inefficient, and in 1867 it was extended to a line between Sullivan and Lenox townships. From time to time it was extended further, and in 1675, the State appropriated $35,000 for its extension and improvement. There was still a lack of drainage and considerable trouble from the volume of water discharged by the canal, and it required another appropriation of $30,000 from the State to complete it.[4] With this, the Douglas Ditch was connected with the Cowaselon Creek, which runs south of the eastern section of the swamp, and which previously had emptied its waters into the swamp. In its course, the Douglas Ditch at the same time provided an outlet for the Canaseraga, which also had emptied its waters into the swamp.

Also, about 1859, the State took another step, when it widened and deepened the Cowaselon Creek. This, eventually, was followed by the building of the Colton Ditch, a commission ditch. This ditch runs through the southeastern portion of the swamp. These improvements aided definitely in the drainage of this land, and it made the swamp "prospectively valuable."[5]

The initial attempt made in the direction of ascertaing the utility of this swamp had happened during the latter 1870's, when a few individuals decided to clear and drain still further a bit of this land in order to test its fertility. Two attempts seem to have occurred simultaneously, both at the edge of the uplands (the dryer spots).

One took place in the southeastern section, or what is now known as Oniontown, the other occurred just off the Main Street road, where the mucklands join the uplands. As soon as onions and celery were sown in these primary plots, success followed immediately.

Clinton Colton and Dewitt Twogood were two of the pioneers in clearing swamplands into productive muck. In the seventies, they began cutting down trees, and little by little, getting small plots in readiness for cultivation. On seeing the success of these first few attempts, others, as usually; happens, began to follow. At first small tracts were cleared, but with the building of secondary ditches these were extended. As has been stated above, this land that was being cleared and made ready for use lay in the dryer sections -- usually near the uplands; and at this same time, progress was possible only in the southeastern end for that section was the only one with adequate drainage. Progress off the Main Street road was hampered because of inadequate drainage.

Another important step in the development of the Mucklands took place when the highway Commissioner of the Town of Lenox decided that that whole section directly north of the village should be transformed from a "water-soaked swamp into a productive area."[6]

Commissioner Foster in 1887, with the approval of the town, began to construct a road through this area (today, this is known as the Oniontown Road). It was at this point that most of the inhabitants of the village really recognized the great possibilities of this territory.

According to the Canastota Bee Journal there were at this time, 1887, about two hundred acres cleared, mostly in the area directly north of the village. Henceforth, clearance and drainage progressed more rapidly; more secondary ditches were built, especially in this section directly north of the village. New roads were constructed and older ones improved. At the same time, more individuals were turning to the mucklands •

By the topographic map of the United States Geological Survey of 1893,[7] we notice that the section directly north of the village (the area between the Main Street and the South Bay roads) was almost entirely drained, and much of it had been cleared and was under cultivation. As many as ten or eleven structures, houses or barns had been built at this time. At the same time, we perceive that the western section of the Canastota Mucklands (that area just south of Gee's Corners) had to a certain extent been drained, but the amount cleared was probably less than in the eastern section. A few attempts had been made to grow vegetables here, but on the whole drainage was still inadequate. With the exception of a few spots along the Main Street Road and a few more along the Pine Ridge Road, which runs east-west immediately to the north of the swamp, the northern and central parts (making up the bulk of the muck area) were still practically untouched. And, what is more, nothing could be done in the direction of development until better drainage, in the form of large ditches, was provided.

At this point, it seems pertinent to stress the difficulty that these pioneers encountered in the process of draining and clearing the land, and also in early cultivation. This work had to be done mostly by hand, with the aid, possibly, of a few horses. Trees had to be cut, the roots dug out, brush and other plants also had to be

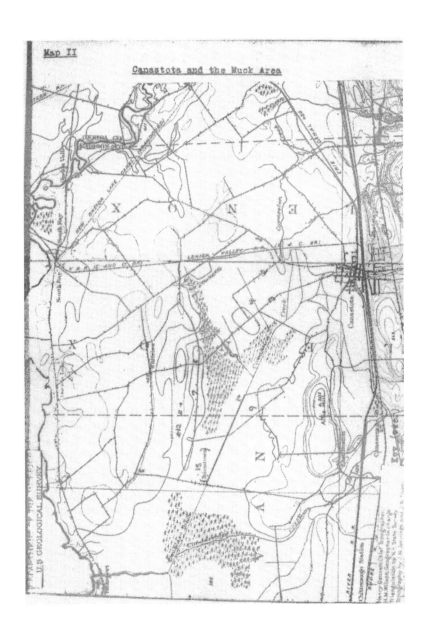

removed, roots and all. Ditches had to be dug entirely by hand. Cultivating this land, when once it had been cleared, must also have been a tremendous job, for there were many roots and other remains which were left behind and which made the surface of the ground very rough. Drainage in some places was good, but others were not so fortunate, and in wet seasons, the growers would find their crops under water. Where drainage was inadequate, there was a great deal of uncertainty, and in some instances the land was abandoned, temporarily.

One of the last important steps, which provided the needed drainage for the central and northern portions, occurred about 1898 when the Child's Ditch was built. With this Commission ditch acting as an outlet, it was now possible to dig many smaller secondary ditches, which were essential at the time. This portion was now, also in readiness for development and work was immediately begun.

At about this time an improvement to the Douglas Ditch provided the essential drainage for the western and southwestern sections, and these sections were now also in line for development.

Thus, by 1900, the foundations for the second largest onion-growing district in the East had been laid. The outlets, in the form or commission ditches sufficient for the drainage of the whole area, had already been constructed. The main outlet of the whole area (the Cowaselon Creek and the Douglas Ditch) had been widened and deepened. Roads to all parts of the area had been laid. All that remained was actual building of the secondary ditches and the work of clearing and preparing the soil for extensive cultivation; and in certain sections, this had already been accomplished.

It is interesting to note, as the names of the pioneers connected with this work are reviewed, that the list is composed entirely of native stock. While it is undoubtedly true that a few of the earlier Italian immigrants of the village were connected in some way with mucklands, either as laborers in clearing the land, or possibly working a bit of it on the share system; it is also true that as far as actual ownership of the land was concerned, before 1900, it rested entirely in the hands of the native stock: Messrs. Twogood, Colton, Wilson, Jennings, Warner, Thackabury, Fisher, Ludlow, Hoffman, Crouse and others.

But, while it may be said that the foundation and the pioneer work for the development of this section was accomplished by the natives of the village, it is at the same time justifiable to hold, as will be shown later, that the actual development and preparation of the soil for extensive cultivation of most of this land must be accredited to the incoming Italians.

V: THE COMING OF THE ITALIANS TO CANASTOTA

Photo Courtesy of the Canastota, New York, Canal Town Museum

Early in his study the writer discovered a very carefully prepared directory of Canastota compiled in 1930. With this and his intimate knowledge of the various Italian families in the town at the time, and aided by contacts with others who had long had close acquaintance with the community, it was not difficult to differentiate by name the 257 Italian families in the village.

Having in mind the historical migration differential from the various portions of Italy, it early became necessary to separate these families by section of Italy In which 'the head of the family (usually the husband) originated.[1]

Since neither the Census material nor the directory supply details regarding these facilities, it became necessary to interview a sizeable sample out of this total of 257. Due to the limited time available and the probable relative homogeneity of the group, it was decided to make an intensive investigation of forty cases distributed in proportions similar (as regards to section of origin) to those in the entire population. Table 5.1 shows the distributions in the entire population, and in the sample.

Careful interviews were undertaken with the head of each household. The particular families were chosen mainly at random, though a few were taken because the writer knew personally the individuals involved, and could in these instances check the information supplied.

Many interesting facts were elicited. Some of the cases are of sufficient interest to warrant their inclusion as life history in the Appendix. The particular lines of questioning are indicated in the "form of Note-taking" (see the Appendix) that was developed prior to the first interview and reduced to final form after a few interviews had suggested changes. Due to the uniformity of their histories, women were not included. Most of the

Table 5.1 Italian Immigrants in Canastota by Section of Origin

Origin[2]	Families	Sample
South Italy	103	16
Sicily	100	13
Central Italy	42	10
Northern Italy	3	1
Unknown	9	0
TOTALS	257	40

women followed the husbands, or they came as part of the families.

One of the most significant sets of facts are the migrational histories of the 40 interviewed. The collective results are the matter of the present chapter. What have been sought are uniformities of behavior rather than statistics. Occasionally, proportions are cited; preponderances are indicated; percentages are studiously avoided.

One of the most important topics is the difference among these sections (according to our sampling) in regards to the time of their departure from Italy. Without any doubt, the first group to leave Italy was the Southern. The departure of those interviewed ranged in years from 1881 to 1913, and two-thirds of these had taken passage before 1906. Somewhat later was the Central Italian group whose range was from 1904 to 1913, with one case coming in 1924. The one, sole Northern Italian case came in 1909. The Sicilians were the last to take their leave from the old country, ranging from 1903 to 1920.

Table 5.2 Departures of Italians from Italy[3]

	Region			
Years	South	Central	Sicilians	North
1880-84	2	0	0	0
1885-89	1	0	0	0
1890-94	0	0	0	0
1895-99	2	0	0	0
1900-04	4	2	2	0
1905-09	5	3	5	1
1910-14	2	4	3	0
1915-19	0	0	1	0
1920-24	0	1	0	0
1925-29	0	0	0	0

With the realization that motivation studies are always most difficult, the next task was an attempt to learn the reasons that led these men to leave their homeland. Little difference was found among the individuals of the various groups in this respect. Keeping in mind the conditions that existed in Italy as given in Chapter 1, it may well be understood why the motive most prevalently given was, "I came to America because

I had heard so many stories of abundance and its opportunities for making money." Many stated that they came to better their economic status. Some, also, had relatives or friends here, and they came to join them.

Comparatively little difference existed among the separate groups as to their intentions of returning to Italy.[4] In about two-thirds of all the cases, leave was taken with the expectation of returning home. Many of them stated that they had planned to stay in America a number of years, make a certain sum of money, return to Italy, and with this money, better their position there. In only about one-third of the cases, or probably less, was there intention, on departure from Italy, of remaining permanently in America.

In coming to the aspect that is most interesting, the Italians and Canastota, the following facts, among others, were investigated. Did these Italian immigrants come directly to Canastota, or did they spend some time in wandering about the country, perhaps settling elsewhere, before coming to Canastota? What were the main factors in this community that acted as a magnet to these people? When did they come? Were there any differences among the various groups?

If the sampling is at all representative of the Italians in this village, it is justifiable to say that by far the majority of Italians, irrespective of the section of Italy they came from, tried their fortune in other parts of the country before coming to Canastota.[5] Due to the type of labor that they were engaged in, and also to the padrone system, many of these men wandered throughout the eastern states, some even penetrating parts of the West. For example, one individual before coming to Canastota had worked in Massachusetts, New York City, the coal mines of Pennsylvania, in the Johnstown area during the flood, and in Syracuse. Another had been in Cortland, Syracuse, Amsterdam, Chicago, Philadelphia, and Auburn. These are by no means exceptions. According to the sampling, about three-quarters visited other parts first, while one-quarter came directly to Canastota.

A fact that is very striking here is that the immediate destination of almost all of these men (exclusive of those that came directly to Canastota) was some large eastern City. This, as has been stated above, is partially explained by the fact that when most of these immigrants disembarked on American shores, they were practically penniless. Thus, they were in dire need of jobs--any kind of a job providing that it brought immediate cash. Only the cities offered opportunities to fulfill these demands, hence the concentration there.

Just as the Southern Italians (of the sample) were the first to depart from their native land, so also were they the first to come to Canastota. The range in years for this group was from 1888 to 1920, but by far the greatest concentration was between the years 1900 to 1915. The Central Italian group seems to have been somewhat slower in settling in this village than the Southern Italians. They ranged in years from 1905 to 1925, but they had their greatest concentration from, 1905 to 1915. The Northern Italians came in 1909. The Sicilians of our sample were the last as a group to come; ranging from 1904 to 1930. The great proportion came from 1905 to 1920. But, as the above figures show, there was no definite cleavage between the groups and naturally, there was a great deal of overlapping. Possibly, if the sampling had been larger, some distinct lines might have been drawn, but unfortunately, time did not

Table 5.3 Arrivals of Italians in Canastota[6]

Years	South	Central	Sicily	North
1885-89	1	0	0	0
1890-94	1	0	0	0
1895-99	0	0	0	0
1900-04	6	0	1	0
1905-09	3	3	2	1
1910-14	3	4	3	0
1915-19	1	1	3	0
1920-24	1	1	3	0
1925-29	0	1	0	0
1930	0	0	1	0

permit that. Regardless, it may be said that the Southern Italians, as a group, were the first to settle in Canastota, while the Sicilians were the last. Why did these immigrants choose Canastota as their abode? This is particularly interesting when it is visualized that the great majority of the Italian immigrants of the time were settling in the larger cities. In dealing this question the problem of motive is again confronted, and again the task is attacked with the realization of the difficulty involved in dealing with and interpreting motives, especially after so many years have lapsed.

But from the facts gathered it seems to have worked out in the following fashion. Previous to 1908 they were coming predominantly in response to the opportunities offered in the village, as explained in Chapter III: that is, labor on the railroads, in the factories, and to a lesser extent by the opportunities for setting up merchant business. During the period 1908 to 1915, a new impetus was added; now, many began to come because of the muckland and its opportunities.[7] During the latter period they were responding to both industry and agriculture. From 1915 to the present the magnet seems to have been predominantly agriculture.

In regards to our cases, for the Southern Italian group which to a great extent was settled in Canastota by 1915, the attraction was almost entirely the railroads and the industrial activities of the village. The same may be said for the Central Italian group with the exception of a few of the later ones who came to raise onions. But, among the Sicilians an altogether different picture is found. From 1908 to the present time they seem to have responded, predominantly, to the opportunities in agriculture. Of course, it is to be understood that many of the Italians that came later had relatives and friends here, and they were persuaded by these friends and relatives to come to Canastota, but something more subtle is sought; for, after all, it would be necessary for these men to earn a living once they arrived.

After this attempt at a classification of the motives for their coming to Canastota, it is of interest to note what the occupations of the individuals of the sampling were at the time of their entrance into the village.

The findings show that the first jobs held by the Southern Italians were in close agreement with the motives in coming to the village given by the group. It was on the railroad and in the shops that they found immediate employment, with a few going into the merchant business. These three categories included all of the cases of this group. Not one individual, in our sampling of these two groups chose agriculture (muck farming) as their immediate means of earning a living. The Sicilians once more offer a striking contrast, for over three-quarters of these went directly onto the muck. This may be partially explained by the fact that the Sicilians were somewhat later in their arrival and the development of the mucklands was a higher level at the time of their greatest migration.

As for transition in occupation among these groups, it was again found that the Southern Italians lead. The facts bear out the point that the majority of this group, sooner or later, left their jobs in the factories and on the railroads and turned to agriculture. In some instances this transition was only temporary, but, as the cases reveal, it is safe to say that the majority in the Southern group have at one time or another engaged in muck farming. There was also a transition among the Sicilians, but it was small and in the direction of agriculture. Those few Sicilians that were not already engaged in muck-farming eventually turned to it. The least transition seems to have taken place among the Central Italians; although many did turn to muck farming, the majority of the cases studied remained at their jobs in the factories and on the railroad. But even a large part of this group has at some time or other worked on the muck farms even though they did not give up their jobs in the village.

There is little doubt that the Sicilians in 1930, as will be shown with evidence in a later section, were the leading element in agriculture. The Southern group was second, while the Central Italians were last.

Table 5.4 Intentions on Departure from Italy[8]

	Return	Remain
Southern	12	4
Central	7	3
Sicilians	12	1
Northern	0	1

Table 5.5 Destinations[9]

	Wandered	Directly
Southern	12	4
Central	5	5
Sicilians	11	2
Northern	0	1

Table 5.6 First Occupations Upon Arrival in Canastota[10]

Table 5.6	Southern	Central	Sicilians	Northern
Shops or Factories	8	4	3	0
Railroad	5	3	0	0
Onion Growing	0	0	10	1
Miscellaneous (Merchants. Barbers, Tailors, others.)	3	3	0	0

Table 5.7 Occupations in 1930[11]

	Southern	Central	Sicilians	Northern
Shops or Factories	4	2	0	0
Railroad	1	2	0	0
Onion Growing	6	1	13[12]	1
Miscellaneous (Merchants. Barbers, Tailors others.)	5	5	0	0

VI: ITALIAN OWNERSHIP OF MUCKLAND

PHOTO COURTESY OF THE CANASTOTA, NEW YORK, CANAL TOWN MUSEUM

At the turn of the present century the foundations for the development of the muck land (as already has been described[1]) were completed, and a good portion of the area was already under cultivation. The need, at this time, was for more labor; for labor that would clear the vast area of newly drained land, and labor that would be willing to work this land when once it was in readiness for operation. Assurance for success in this occupation was not lacking, and the Italians, who in the majority of cases had come from agricultural districts of Italy, were not long in responding to this opportunity.

Most of the Italians, according to the sampling, had

departed from Italy with the expectancy of returning after a few years.[2] But some of them must have dispensed with this notion early for when they arrived in the village, they not only began to establish residence there, but as soon as they had enough money, they began to buy mucklands.

In a very interesting and fascinating manner these Italians began, slowly at first but later with increasing rapidity, to obtain a firm foothold on these fertile lands. By way of analysis of this movement an attempt will be made to trace the increase of Italian ownership on the mucklands by five-year intervals -- from 1900 when there was not a single acre owned by an Italian to 1930 when a good deal more than half of the approximate 2,500 acres under cultivation was in their hands.

Although ownership is to be the main factor under discussion, this does not imply that those Italians buying land were the first or the only ones engaged in agriculture at the time. In fact, very few purchased land immediately on their first contact with it. In other words, most of them went through what might be called an apprenticeship period. Before buying, there were a number of procedures that an Italian might follow. For instance, many went about it in this fashion: first they would obtain about three or four acres from the native owner, which the Italian with his family proceeded to work on the share-system. But in order to have the means with which to buy the necessities needed during this time one of the family, usually the father, would be engaged in day labor. He might be working in a factory, on the railroads or, as often happened, he might be hired by another muck owner to help clear land. After a time the immigrant would desire a larger plot, so he usually took his family to another farm where they were allotted more acreage. This also was to be worked on the share-system. This continued until the immigrant found a patch that was sufficient for him and his family, or until he had decided to buy land of his own.[3] Some of the Italians worked the share-system for only a few years before buying; many were in it for a much longer period, while others (including some of the early comers) are still at it today.

An Italian might have bought land that was totally cleared, or that was only partially cleared. Some purchased land that was totally uncleared. If the farm was only partially cleared, the immigrant and his family would plant and work the part that was cleared, but at the same time they would slowly be putting the rest of it in readiness for cultivation. Much of the work of clearing these lands was also done by these people during the fall and winter after the onion season.

Thus, while there was a gradual turnover from native ownership to alien, there were at the same time, other Italians who were clearing land and raising onions or celery on the share-system. And the general opinion is that it was not until after the war that the amount of land owned was more than the amount that was being operated on the share-system by the Italians.

Before proceeding to the task of tracing Italian ownership of muck, one distinction is necessary. While this area under consideration is really one continuous stretch, it is divided politically by a township line, which runs north and south through it.[4] The approximate three-quarters of the area lying to the east of the line is in the Town of Lenox, while the western one-quarter is in the Town of Sullivan.[5] Though this division will be used in the analysis in an effort to weigh the increase of ownership in one section as against the other, it is essential to keep in mind the fact that the territory is only theoretically divided.

The figures representing Italian ownership of mucklands and Italian owners (which will follow presently) were computed by the writer from the Tax Records of the towns of Lenox and Sullivan --the area in which this land lies. The procedure used was to go through the records of the particular years in question, pick out the Italian owners and the amount of muckland owned. In a number of oases the type of land was not specified, but because of the fact that very few Italians have ever owned anything but muckland, and because most of them still own the same farms it was not difficult to determine the type of land. In a few instances (to act as a check-up) the writer went to the owners themselves and obtained the required information. The only difficulty that was encountered was with the few owners that possessed both upland and muckland, that is, where no specification was made.

Although a small number of Italians were already engaged in the operation of onion farms on the share-system,[6] actual ownership did not begin until 1902, when Michael Patterelli bought a five-acre plot from Lucretia Thackabury.[7] This first purchase occurred in the Town of Lenox. Since this land was not developed, Patterelli with the assistance of his family set about to clear it.

By 1905 three other Italians had made purchases. During this interval both Libero Valerio and Michael Bush[8] had bought a ten-acre plot each, while John Cerio purchased fifteen acres. At this time these four immigrants were in possession of 40 acres, and all of it lay in the Town of Lenox.

In the following five-year interval there was a substantial increase in ownership, so that by 1910 there were a total of 21 proprietors holding about 167 acres. The average acreage per holding was 7.9 acres. But this growth had occurred almost completely in the Lenox area, and only one farm -- of eleven acres -- had been purchased in the Sullivan area. Evidently, progress in the development of the latter area was still slow or else the distance from the village made the Italians hesitant, at least, in so far as buying land was concerned. For along with ownership there came a number of responsibilities and burdens, which the share-worker did not have to face. The more serious of these were housing, means of communication, and the transportation of crops. This section is the furthest in distance from the village.

Sixteen additional immigrants became proprietors during the period between 1910 and 1915. Thus, at the latter date a total of 37 families were in possession of about 341 acres. The average acreage per holding was 9.2 acres. During this period the turnover in the Sullivan area showed increased activity. In this area, nine immigrant Italians and their families had about 125 acres. While 28 in the Lenox section cultivated about 216 acres.

During the next five-year interval, when the Sicilian movement was in full swing, the total number of owners more than doubled while the acreage multiplied almost three-fold. To state this in figures, by 1920 there were 88 Italians owning farms and these amounted to about 913 acres. The average acreage per holding had risen somewhat and was now about 10.3 acres. The surprising fact about this period was that the principle increase -- in both number of holdings and the acreage -- occurred in the heretofore slower Sullivan area. During this period there was a comparatively immense increase of 33 new owners making a total of 42 proprietorships, while its acreage of 518 surpassed that of the Lenox area. In the latter section the increase was not so rapid. Forty-six families now possessed about 395 acres. The increase in the Sullivan area was probably due to the activity of the Sicilian group. Both the area south of Gee's Corners and the Indian Opening Section were now in full swing and both of these areas have always been predominantly operated by Sicilians. But only further investigation could prove this point.

Table 6.1 Italian Muck Owners in Lenox and Sullivan Compared[9]

Year	Average Acreage Per Holding		Total Acreage Owned By Italians		Number of Italians Owning Farms	
	Lenox	Sullivan	Lenox	Sullivan	Lenox	Sullivan
1902	5	0	5	0	1	0
1905	10	0	40	0	4	0
1910	7.8	11	156	11	20	1
1915	7.7	13.8	216	125	28	9
1920	8.5	12.3	395	518	46	42
1925	10.1	12.2	961	600	95	49
1930	9.6	10.5	1000	610	103	52

Table 6.2 Total Muck Owners and Acreage[10]

Year	Number of Italians Owning Farms	Average Acreage Per Holding	Total Acreage Owned By Italians
1902	1	5	5
1905	4	10	40
1910	21	7.9	167
1915	37	9.2	341
1920	88	10.3	913
1925	144	10.8	1,561
1930	155	10.4	1,610

The greatest increase, in reality, took place during the first five years of the following decade. During this interim there occurred an additional increase of 56 owners. Thus, by 1925, the number of Italian-American owners was 144 and they had accumulated approximately 1,560 acres. The average holding was now 10.8 acres. Again there was a reversal in regard to the situation in the two sections involved. In this instance it was the Lenox area that was responsible for the tremendous increase. The Lenox owners not only had doubled in number, but there was a huge increase in the amount of land owned. The number of proprietors in this section now stood at 95 and they controlled about 961 acres --

an increase or almost 600 acres. Progress in the Sullivan section was much slower and 49 owners possessed about 600 acres.

In the period of national prosperity immediately preceding the Depression the increase in Italian-American ownership was relatively slight. In 1930 a total of 155 families -- and an increase of only eleven -- were in possession of about 1,610 acres in both areas. The average acreage per holding remained approximately the same, about 10.4 acres. Lenox now had 103 owners possessing about 1,000 acres, while Sullivan's total of 52 owners operated about 608 acres.

Of course, it is to be understood that by this time the Italians were in possession of a good deal more than half of the lands under cultivation, and, as has been stated previously, it probably was some time directly after the war, or in the early twenties that the halfway mark was reached and surpassed. Not only did the Italian-Americans now own most of this land but also practically the whole area was being operated by them, if not by direct ownership, then through the share-system. This change to complete Italian-American operation is difficult to trace for no facts are available. The opinion is that it probably took place around 1910. From that time on operation was almost totally in the hands of the immigrants and their children; and as time passed and more and more Italians came in, they cleared, cultivated and bought more and more land.

One peculiarity that needs further comment is the size of the holdings, or farms, of the Italians. The original owners of the land possessed large tracts; always of fifty, sixty or more acres. But, though there are a few large farms among the immigrants, most of them have small holdings ranging anywhere from four to fifteen acres. The average acreage per holding, as may be seen from the figures just presented, never exceeded eleven acres.

The reason for these small farms lies in a number of factors. One is the fact that a small plot of about ten acres when planted with onions, celery, carrots, lettuce, or any otter vegetable has to be hand worked and requires an astonishing amount of labor -- even for a good-sized industrious family. Another factor that played an important part was that this land is comparatively expensive. When the Italians first started to buy land it was much cheaper, costing anywhere from $30 to $100 per acre, but today it is worth from $300 to $800 per acre; depending naturally, on the locality, fertility, and means of communication and transportation.[11] A small holding of this size (10 acres) is also, usually, sufficient for the sustenance of practically any family. For normally such a plot will bring close to $3,000 per year, if not more.

VII: THE POPULATION OF CANASTOTA[1]

Photo Courtesy of the D'Amico Family

In an effort to analyze the population of Canastota, as complete a picture as possible has been drawn by collecting all of the available authoritative statistics on the subject. These findings are presented in a basic form in tables 7.1 through 7.2.2. For various reasons the figures on the Italian population for 1890 or before are not available, but it is rather doubtful if the number could have been in any way significant at that time. In only one instance was difficulty encountered, and that was in obtaining the statistics for the native white of foreign or mixed parentage with at least one parent born in Italy for the year 1920. But, though the actual numbers were not available, there was sufficient material available otherwise to enable a good estimate to be made.

As may be gathered from Table 7.1, there was a gradual increase in the total population of Canastota from 1890 to 1930, this being the period that witnessed practically the entire Italian movement. In 1890, by the United States Census report, Canastota's population was set at 2,774, and in every succeeding decade until 1930, when the population was 4,235 (a gain of 1,461) there was an increase ranging from 200 to 250 with one exception. This exception being the World War decade (1910-1920), when there was an addition of 748. An attempt to account for this gain will be made a little later.

The native white population of native parentage fluctuated somewhat during this time; though, all in all, it gained somewhat in number, but in proportion to the total population of the village there was an appreciable decrease. In 1890 there were 2,000 native whites of native parentage and these composed 73 percent of the total population. In 1900 the native whites of native parentage were still responsible for 72 percent or the total. But in 1910, when the village population was 3,247, the proportion of native white of native parentage was 61 percent -- a decrease of 11 percent. No doubt this proportionate decrease was due primarily to the coming of a large number of foreign-born Italians. The proportion continued to drop, and in 1920 it was 59 percent. The cause for this continued drop at this point can be attributed to the second generation Italian. At the time of the last census (1930), when the total population of the village was placed at 4,235, the amount of the native white of native parentage group was 2,324 or 55 percent. Thus, in no way is it possible to attribute the comparatively large increase in the Canastota population to the native population.

In respect to the figure for the foreign born Italians, it is seen that there was a steady increase from 1900 to 1930. At the former date, there were in the village, 58 Italians and these represented only 2 percent of the population. By 1910 the number had risen to 281 and 9 percent of the total. Incidentally, more Italians established residence in Canastota during this decade than in any other -- 223 in number. During the following decade 184 additional Italians came to Canastota to establish residence, so that by 1920 there were 465 foreign born Italians. They now composed 12 per cent of the total population of the village. The twenties did not witness such a rapid increase and in 1930, the 525 foreign-born Italians made up 10 per cent of whole. Henceforth, because Italian immigration to the United States has almost completely stopped, and because the Italian foreign born are reaching the upper stages of life, their proportion and their number in the village will probably decline steadily. But here, the fact that migration from other parts of the United States may occur has been disregarded. If a sizeable migration should occur the number would probably increase.

As should be expected, the males among the Italians foreign-born groups have always been in excess of the females. This is explained by the 'fact that for a time Italian immigration was one predominantly of males.[2] In 1900, of the 58 foreign-born Italians in Canastota there were almost three males for every female. This is a high proportion but not unusual to the total Italian population in the country at that time. During the 1900-1910 decade the males were beginning to send to Italy for their wives who they had left behind, and at the end of this period a much larger number of females was found, so that by 1910 there were 162 males per 100 females. In the World War decade the number of females coming to Canastota actually surpassed the males. In 1920 there were 126 males per 100 females. Following this, the proportion remained the same. That is, in 1930 there were 293 males and 232 females or, 126 males per 100 females.

Canastota's Population[3]

Table 7.1 Population Totals

Year	Male	Female	TOTAL
1930	2095	2140	4235
1920	1934	2061	3995
1910	1615	1632	3247
1900	1541	1489	3030
1890	1378	1396	2774

Table 7.1.1 Native Born Whites

Year	Of Native Parents TOTALS	Of Foreign or Mixed Parentage		TOTAL
		Italians	Others	
1930	2324	879	360	1239
1920	2342	600	427	1027
1910	2126	155	459	614
1900	2167	26	517	543
1890	2000			427

Table 7.1.2 Foreign Born Whites

Year	Italians	Others	TOTAL
1930	525	133	658
1920	465	144	609
1910	281	184	465
1900	58	222	280
1890			308

Table 7.2 First and Second Generation Italians in the Canastota Population[4]

Year	Male	Female	TOTAL
1930	716	688	1404
1920			1065[5]
1910	253	183	436
1900	52	32	84

Table 7.2.1 Foreign Born Italians in the Canastota Population

Year	Male	Female	TOTAL
1930	293	232	525
1920	260	205	465
1910	174	107	281
1900	43	15	58

Table 7.2.2 Native Born Italians in the Canastota Population with Foreign Born or Mixed Parentage

Year	Male	Female	TOTAL
1930	423	456	879
1920			600
1910	79	76	155
1900	9	17	26

A rapid increase took place among the native white of foreign or mixed parentage[6] (at least one parent Italian). This increase was especially pronounced between 1910 and 1930. During this interval the number rose from 155 to 879, an increase of 724, or 387 percent. In particular, the World War decade with an addition of 445 witnessed the heaviest growth, among these second generation Italians. To this increase, most of the credit for the growth in the total population of the village during this period, previously mentioned, maybe attributed. This clearly shows that it was only after the Italian immigrant had settled in the village that the second generation began to multiply.

It is only when the foreign born and the second generation Italians are combined that the largest increase is seen. In 1900 the total of this combination number 84, or only three percent of the village's total population. Henceforth, a substantial increase took place in every decade. In the year 1910 the total first and second generation Italians amounted to 436 or 13 percent of the whole population. The following decade saw an addition of more than 600, and in 1920 approximately 1,065 persons of Italian extraction represented 26 percent of the total population of the village. Thus, by 1930, the number of Canastotans of Italian extraction[7] amounted to 1,404. They composed 30 per cent of the total population.

An increase to some extent is seen in all the different elements of the population with two exceptions. The first exception is the foreign born group of other than Italian origin. In this element a steady decrease took place. By the Census of 1890 there was a total of 308 foreign born of all nationalities in the village, and there is reason to believe that little less than 300 were other than Italians. By 1900 the total foreign born had declined to 280, but of these only 58 were Italians. That is, about 21 percent of the foreign groups were Italians while the remaining 79 percent were other than Italians.

With the coming of the Italians in large numbers during the first decade of the twentieth century, the total number of foreign-born naturally increased, and at the end of this decade (1910) they numbered 465. But of these, now, only 184 or 40 percent were non-Italians. This decline continued and in 1920 their number of 144 represented only 25 percent of the total foreign born. The last census reported this group to be 133, or about 21 percent of the foreign element. The Italian foreign group, at this time, totaled 525, or 19 percent of the 658 total foreign born. The other exception was the native white of foreign or mixed parentage with parents other than Italians.

For a summarization of this population analysis --it is seen that the population of Canastota increased from 3,030, in 1900 to 4,235 in 1930, a gain of 1,205. How can this gain be accounted for -- if it is to be accounted for at all? The native white of native parentage group while not actually decreasing in number can hardly be said to have made any great substantial gain. The foreign born group of other than Italian parentage actually declined, as did the second generation of this group. The only alternative remaining is to conclude that the Italians, both first and second generation, were mainly responsible for the increase in the population of Canastota.

As an added interest, a map depicting the distribu-

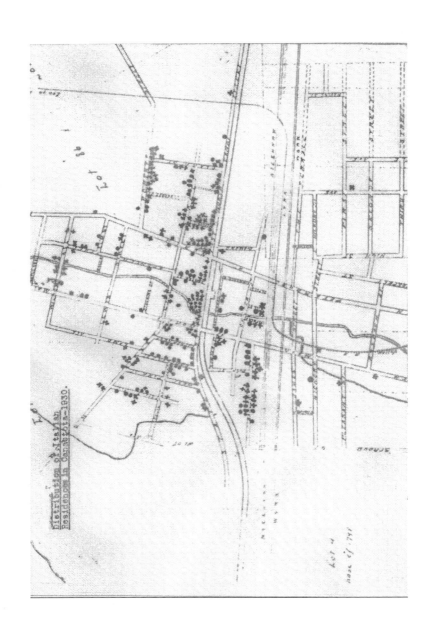

tion of residences of the Italians of this village in 1930 shows that almost the entire Italian group resided, at this time, north of the railroads. In particular there seemed to be a heavy concentration north of the Erie Canal, especially along the Canal itself and on the streets adjacent to it. At the same time, there seemed to be little difference as to the residence of the agricultural Italians and those that found employment in the industries of the village or elsewhere. These two groups seemed to be evenly distributed throughout the northern part of the village, with the exception that the section between South State and New Boston Street undoubtedly had a surplus of agricultural Italians, while Roberts Street was inhabited predominantly by non-muck farmers. This, it must be remembered, was the situation in 1930; without any doubt many changes have occurred since that time.

VIII: THE ITALIANS IN AGRICULTURE

Photo Courtesy of the Canastota, New York, Canal Town Museum

Farming Methods

Although the onion is not the only vegetable grown on the mucklands, it is by far the most prevalent and the most important. In the South "Cotton is King" but here "Onion is King." For this reason, this description of farming method will be done only as it pertains to the onion-growing phase.

The most logical point from which to begin the description of this system seems to be the springtime and the planting season. After the muck owner has had his land plowed (this may be done in the fall after the harvest or in the spring) it is "dragged", fertilizer is applied, and then it is smoothed over. With this, the preparation of the land for planting is completed. The actual planting usually takes place in April, or occasionally in the first part of May. The types of onions that may be grown are two, seed and set onions. The seed onions are grown from the actual seeds of the plant, while set onions are grown from very small onion bulbs, which have to be transplanted.[1] The seed onions are planted by hand-operated machines in rows 12 or 14 inches apart. In planting sets, a different method is used. The transplanting of these little bulbs by machines has been attempted often, but the onion grower because these planters will drop the bulbs upside down, sideward, or too thick believes that satisfactory results are not obtainable. So, the transplanting is usually performed by hand labor. That is, these small bulbs are set into the ground one by one, by individuals on their hands and knees; a real back-breaking task. The rows, in this case are 12 or 14 inches apart, and are marked out beforehand.

    The length of time required for the seedlings to appear above ground depends, naturally, on the weather conditions, but usually it takes about two weeks for the seed onions, and one for the sets.

    With the appearance of the young plants above

ground, a period of cultivation and weeding sets in. The former task is accomplished by cultivators, which are hand operated. Weeding, which is probably the most irksome job in the onion growing business is done practically in the same fashion as transplanting, that is, on hands and knees. Cultivation and weeding covers in the case of seed onions a period of about three months; while for the set onions, which mature earlier, is about two months. After this, there is a short period during which little work is attempted. In this interval the stalk begins to dry up and fall while the onion begins to mature.

During the last part of July the harvesting season commences. At this time, the Italian-American farmers and their families begin to pull the set onions and lay them in row on the ground. The work of pulling onions is accomplished completely by hand, and it is difficult to imagine how it could be done otherwise. As soon as the tops are dried by the sun, the worker comes along and clips them one by one, at the same time, putting them in crates. The same is done with the seed onions when they mature -- about a month later. Machines for the purpose of clipping onions do exist,[2] but since they usually damage the large bulbs, they are used only occasionally.

Lastly, the onions are sold, screened (cleaned), and bagged, or they are trucked to the village and stored.

The usual method is to sell part of the crop on the land, and store the remainder in hopes of obtaining better prices in the winter.

The Share-System:

The share-system in use on the muck farms has never developed into the complicated and discouraging system that is found in the South among the cotton growers. The system as used by the Italian-Americans here, has always been both simple and beneficial for the two parties concerned. Often, no contract is drawn up between the two for an understanding is sufficient.

Technically the system varies from time to time and from owner to owner, but in essentials it is the same everywhere. One Italian-American youth who in the same number of years has grown onions for three different owners on the share-system reported the system in essential, as far as he knew it, to be as follows.[3] The owner fits the land entirely. That is, the responsibility of preparing the land for planting lies entirely in his hands. The owner must furnish all the implements that this type of farming requires. Usually he also furnishes the fertilizer. The cost of the seeds and the "little sets" to be used for transplantation are split by the two parties concerned. This, usually, is the only instance in which the share-worker is required to make any payment. But, the work involved in growing the crop is borne entirely by the share-worker. He and his family must do the planting, cultivating, weeding, pulling, and clipping. After the onions are clipped and put into crates, the crop is theoretically divided then and there, but usually on agreement they continue to work together. That is, the owner furnishes transportation for the whole crop, while the share-worker continues to do the work involved. Finally, the proceeds from the crop are divided equally between the two.

If the worker is to live on the farm during the summer, housing facilities are furnished by the owner, and these are free of rent for the share-worker.

As one may well see, the terms under the share-system very satisfactory to the worker, all that he usually has to furnish is the labor and half the cost of the seed. And with this he is entitled to half of the proceeds of the crop. To show that this system has always been profitable to the Italian immigrants one has only to realize that the gap to ownership is almost inevitably passed by the use of this system. It is by the use of this system that the Italian can save enough so that he may be able to buy his own land. After the harvest season is over the share-workers is at liberty to leave the land or he may remain.

Vegetables Grown

There was a time when celery was almost as important a crop as onions, but as the years advanced and growers relied on onions to a greater extent than ever before, there has been a great reduction in the acreage devoted to celery.[4] At the present time, though the amount of land devoted to celery is far from the amount given over to onions, it is still without any doubt the second most important crop.

Lettuce, though not finding as strong a market as in past years, is still grown in large quantities. Carrots and potatoes are also raised to some extent. But, as the Canastota Bee Journal reports, "the exuberant, odoriferous onion is king."

Labor

It has been stated before that intensive cultivation such as this requires a great deal of labor. This is especially true in certain wet seasons, when the weeds seem to spring as fast as one can pull them. The onion crop requires constant labor from the time it is planted to the harvest season. If the Italian onion grower had had to hire labor to help work his land, it is a gamble as to the amount of success that he would have attained. The one great reason for his success lies, doubtlessly, in the fact that no outside labor was required, or at least none was used. The onion grower utilized the labor of his family to the fullest extent. The wife as well as the children labored day in and day out. Summer was no vacation for the school children, but a period during which their natural desires were almost completely restrained. During rush periods hours were long and tedious, and 10 to 12 hours of backbreaking labor a day was nothing uncommon. If school was in session, the children would have to hurry home after school, change to overalls and work until dusk.

During the present decade matters seem to be taking a different turn. The labor of wives is less in evidence.[5] Even the labor of children is less common. Hours of work per day are shorter. Evening after evening is no longer spent monotonously on the farm, but with the common usage of motor vehicles, these people are able to find outlets in the activities or the village.

There also seems to be at the present time a trend toward the hiring of mass labor. For instance, during the planting and harvesting seasons, due to the fact that the labor from the village is insufficient, many or the growers send their trucks to the nearby cities of Oneida, Utica, Rome, and even Syracuse for mass help. Recently, a number of Negroes from other parts of the country have been found working for the Italians during these seasons.

Communication And Housing

In the past the Italian onion grower of Canastota has usually been a person with two habitats.[6] In the winter be made his home in the village, but as soon as spring rolled around he would pack up all the essentials and move to the farm. Here he remained throughout the onion season. A small number of muck farmers lived permanently in the village and commuted to work daily. It must be remembered that at this time the automobile was not a common phenomenon among these immigrants, and due to the distance of the village from the fields of labor it was absolutely necessary for most of these people to establish residence on the muck farms during the summer months.

In the last decade, with the common usage or the automobile, a change in the above situation has also taken place. Although there still are a number who move to the farm lands for the summer months; by far the greater part abide continuously in the village and commute to work daily. This allows the Italian-American farmers and their families to keep in constant touch with the village and to enjoy its benefits the year round. At the same time they are able to operate their farms as effectively as ever. Very few of these families are without a motor vehicle, be it truck or auto. Many possess both. In case a family cannot afford a car or a large truck, they, at least, possess a "muck truck." These muck trucks are usually made simply by obtaining an old Dodge Brothers vehicle,[7] stripping off the body, and building a rack on it. These trucks are used for all purposes. They are used in place of tractors; at least in so far as transporting crops off the soft mucklands is concerned. They are used as road trucks and they are also used as motorcars. Practically every onion growing family possesses at least one.

Almost every muck owner possesses a house on his land. And in the case of large farms where a number of share-workers are required, a house is available for every worker and family on that farm. For example, the Klockdale Farm, one of the largest onion farms in operation, has as many as six houses for its workers.

The houses of these people are usually found along the roads. These homes are of various types. Many are two-story structures, and these usually are winter-proof. Some are of the bungalow fashion, while others are just plain shanties.

Seasonality Of Muck Agriculture

As probably has been gathered, onion farming is a seasonable task. It commences usually in April and ends in early fall or sooner. During late fall and winter no work is required on the land, and with the exception of selling and bagging the onions that have been stored, there is little work in connection with the business itself. A discussion of winter work will be found in the following chapter.

Number Of Italian Families In Agriculture[8]

There were approximately 257 Italian families

having residence in Canastota in 1930, and of this number about 153 were dependent on agriculture for a livelihood. These Italian farmers were 67 per cent of the whole group of Italian families.

The predominant group in agriculture, as was intimated in Chapter V, is the Sicilian. This group in 1930 was found to have about 100 families[9] in the village and of these 86 were muck farmers. The Southern Italian families numbered about 103; 48 or 47 per cent were onion growers. The Central Italian group had about 42 families in the village, at that time, and of these only 14 or 33 percent were onion farmers. All of the three Northern Italian families found were agriculturalists.

Table 8.1 Comparative Numbers of Italian Families in Agriculture – 1930[10]

Native Region	Onion Growers	Other Occupations	TOTAL
Southern Italians	48	55	103
Sicilians	86	14	100
Northern Italians	3	0	3
Central Italians	14	28	42
Unknown	2	7	9
TOTALS	153	104	257

IX: ITALIANS IN OTHER OCCUPATIONS

Photo Postcard Courtesy of Thomas R. D'Amico

In the previous chapter[1] it was seen that about two-thirds of the Italian families of Canastota in 1930 gave their occupations as onion growers. This means that the remaining one-third, or 104, was employed otherwise. In reference to the separate groups the central Italians had the lowest proportion in agriculture and correspondingly the highest proportionate number in other occupations. That is, of the approximate 42 Central Italian families about 28 or two-thirds made a living through other occupations. The South Italian group also bad a larger number in occupations other than agriculture, but in this case, the distribution was almost equal.

There were about 103 families of this group and 55 or a little more than half were in non-agricultural occupations. The majority of the Sicilians, as has been stated previously, were workers of the soil. Approximately 100 families of this group had residence in Canastota in 1930, and of this number only 14 were found in occupations other than agriculture.

It probably would be of interest to determine what these other occupations in which the Italians found employment were. Again this was made possible by the use of the Canastota Classified Directory of 1930. In Table 9.1 a classification of the different occupations for the various groups of foreign-born Italians with male as heads of families bas been attempted. From this, it is seen that outside of agriculture most of the Italians, as would be expected were employed on the railroads and in factories. Of the two, the railroad seemed to employ the most -- 32 in number. Factory labor, skilled and unskilled, drew about 28 foreign born Italian. The skilled laborers, numbering 18 were mostly cabinetmakers, woodworkers, and upholsters. There were also, at this time about 15 merchants. These included grocers, butchers, tailors, and shoe merchants. Besides these, there was a slight scattering in other occupations: plumbers, day laborers, painters, salesmen, mechanics, fruit dealers, onion buyers and others. In all these totaled 21 and in Table 9.1 are placed in the category termed miscellaneous.

Breaking this up into the different Italian groups, it was found that there were more Southern Italians working on the railroads than any other group. To be more specific, there were 19 South Italians working on the railroads in 1930, six Central Italians, and only two Sicilians. The same is true for the factory workers; the South Italians led with 13, the Central Italians bad eight in this category, while the Sicilians had only five. There were also more South Italian merchants.

It has been stated that muck farming is a seasonable task, and that during the late fall and winter months-the onion grower, except for the little attention that might be needed for the onion he has stored, has little to do. What do these Italian-Americans do during this interval? The answer to this question is drawn chiefly from observation, and also from the opinions of a number of individuals.

A number of these growers possess large trucks and, as soon as the shipping period starts they promptly enter the trucking business. They freight onions to practically all the large cities of the East. A small number are employed as buyers for large produce firms. A few find part-time employment on the railroads. At the present time, since factory labor is usually at a very low ebb during the winter, very few are able to obtain employment in factories or shops. Many find frequent but sporadic work in helping other owners "screen" stored onions. But many of them, undoubtedly, do very little besides taking full advantage of their membership in one or both of the two Italian societies in the village. The clubrooms of the Italian-American Citizen Club and of the Society of S. Egidio Abbate are used as places for meeting, discussion and by some as places for hibernation.

Table 9.1 Distribution of Male Heads of Families in Groups and Occupation in 1930[2]

	Southern Italians	Sicilians	Central Italians	Northern Italians	Unknown	TOTALS
Muck Farmers	48	86	14	3	2	153
Railroad Workers	19	2	6	0	5	32
Factory Workers	13	5	8	0	2	28
Merchant	7	3	5	0	0	15
Misc.	10	4	7	0	0	21
Unknown/Retired	6	0	2	0	0	8
TOTALS	103	100	42	3	9	257

X: CONCLUSION

Photo Courtesy of Samuel J. D'Amico

This study is by no means complete. Furthermore it does not propose to be an exhaustive analysis of the community. Because of lack of time, and not interest, many aspects both interesting and important have had to be omitted. Also, many of the topics which were discussed could be expanded to include more details and particulars.

Since many aspects of this community have not been investigated, the writer would like to think of this thesis as an instigation for further study. Future students, as well as others, will find it to their interest and benefit to study some of the phases that have been neglected. With this in mind, a number of recommendations for investigation will be made.

Especially enlightening would be a study of the social, religious, educational, and political life of these Italians. An equally stimulating topic would be one that dealt with culture and custom -- emphasizing the carry-over from Italy and the impact of American institutions.

Because of the fact that little was said of hardships and nothing of failures among these people, one might derive the notion that these do not exist. Nothing could be further from the truth. But all were able to adjust themselves satisfactorily to this manner of living. Some, even, were forced to abandon their attempt at onion growing. Aside from this, no cognizance was taken of the fact that many of the muck-owners have, undoubtedly, incurred heavy mortgages.

An important inclusion in any further study would be one that dealt with the labor on the muckland. It is obvious that when the Italians first came to Canastota their labor was exploited by the American owners. Somewhat later, as the Italians began to buy land and work the share-system more and more, they in turn, exploited the labor of their families. At the present time, another change has taken place. Now the Italians are beginning to exploit outside labor.

In dealing with the population of the village, this

thesis, for obvious reasons was not able to go beyond 1930. But with the publication of the census of 1940 and possibly of a classified Canastota Directory, material will be available for someone to record the changes that have taken place during the last decade. Two other fields that would require special study by themselves are the effects of the depression on the Italians, and the second generation Italians.

APPENDIX

Photo Courtesy of Samuel J. D'Amico

Case I - Mike[1]

Mike is a Southern Italian, coming from the village of Compochiano in the province of Molise. Before coming to America Mike was a mulester receiving very low wage. At that time, many of his fellow villagers who were in America were sending money back home. This, as much as anything else, helped Mike to make his decision.

In 1888, at the age of 22, Mike forsook Italy for America. His wife and two children were left behind for he intended to return home after a short sojourn. On reaching America, he immediately entrained for Massachusetts where he was employed on a railroad construction job. After a number of months, be left for Corning, New York. His work in Corning took the form of sewage construction. Continuing his wandering, Mike next went to Pittston, Pennsylvania, where he obtained work in the coal mines. But after a day's work, he decided that mining was not to his liking and he returned to Corning to labor on a railroad. After the Johnstown flood Mike was to be found repairing damaged railroad tracks.

Syracuse was Mike's next destination. Here he worked in the Soda Ash Works, and later on the West Shore Railroad. While in Syracuse this immigrant broke all existing ties with the "old country." In the first place, he sent for his wife and children whom he had left In Italy. And then in 1893, after his waiting period of five years had expired, Mike was granted his American citizenship papers.[2]

In 1894, one of Mike's friends brought him to Canastota and aided him in obtaining employment on what is now the Lehigh Valley R.R. for $1.00 a day. Soon, this was abandoned 1n favor of work on the West

Shore line at $1.25 a day. Soon the New York Central R.R. was offering $1.35 per day and Mike again changed job. Mike has worked on railroads for more than 30 years.

Shortly after 1896 Mike bought a home in the Village. This was one of the two first purchases to be made in the village of Canastota by an Italian immigrant.[3]

In 1902, Mike bought a five-acre farm on the mucklands. This being the first purchase of muck by an Italian. This land was not prepared for cultivation and since Mike was working on the railroad at the time, most of the task of cleaning the land was done on Sundays. After this, for many years, Mike continued his employment on the railroad while the family took care of the onion crop. Not so many years ago, Mike was an agent for a number of large seed firms.

At the present time, though possessing neither house nor land, Mike is retired.

Case II - Salvatore[4]

The birthplace of Salvatore was in the city of Castiglione, on the Island of Sicily. His father was a vineyard owner. Salvatore, as a youth, was not required to help his father, so he soon found employment elsewhere. Previous to his departure for America, Salvatore had been employed as an overseer. For his services he was receiving but 23 cents a day. Regular laborers were paid one lire (20 cents) a day.

Naturally, Salvatore was dissatisfied with the conditions that he was forced to live in. The rumors and stories that came to him concerning America were almost unbelievable. He was told that in America good jobs were plentiful and wages were high. So, when he was 25 years old, he decided that he would try his fortune in America. His intentions at the time were to go to America, remain a number of years, or at least until he had earned a certain amount of money, and then with this he would return home to his young wife who he was leaving behind.

Salvatore set sail for the United States in 1906. A short time later he found himself in New York City. But his stay in this metropolis was brief, for he immediately departed for Bennington, Vermont with a group of paisons (fellow villagers). Here, be worked on a railroad construction job for 22 months. Then, with the same group, he returned to New York City, where he found employment in a coal yard. After a few months of this, he left for Newburgh to work in a brickyard.

Almost three years had now lapsed since his departure from Italy, and on pleas from his wife be returned to the "old country" in 1908. While working in America he had sent money to his wife. And on his return be carried 1,000 lire ($200) home with him.

In 1910, Salvatore decided to come to America again; this time with his wife and children. The wife's oldest sister, who had established residence in Canastota, persuaded the two young immigrants to come to this vlllage. They were told of the fine opportunities for work in the village, and also about the mucklands. On arrival in the village, Salvatore immediately found work as a bridge builder. But the two remained in Canastota only a short time, for they soon returned to New York City. There they remained for the winter of 1910-11. Now no work was obtainable during this time, and they soon decided to return to Canastota. When they arrived in the village, for the second time, they immediately began to work nine acres of muckland on the share-system. At the same time Salvatore worked on construction jobs.

Salvatore and his family raised onions on the share-system until 1922. During all this time he had entertained hopes of returning to Italy. In fact, he even sent money to that country to be deposited. But, by 1922 hopes of ever returning had faded away, and he bought a 13-acre muck farm. In the same year be also purchased a home in the village.
Since that time, he has bought more land in the village. At the present time Salvatore operates his onion farm.

Case III - Sergio[5]

This individual was born in the province of Marche in Central Italy. Until be was 25 years old he worked for his father, who made a reasonable living by maintaining a machine shop. At about this time Sergio's mother died. And as he himself stated, "I was disgusted with everything." Though he had not heard very much about America he decided in 1913, to come here. He departed with no intentions of returning.

Sergio, also, had a friend in Canastota with whom he corresponded. Naturally, this friend told him of the opportunities that the village offered. Sergio came directly to Canastota, and because of the fact that he had bad experience in his father's shop; he immediately found work in the Lenox Shop as a skilled laborer.

After working here for a number of years he moved to Cortland, remaining in that city for one year and a half. At the end of this period he trekked back to Canastota and again back to skilled labor.

Since this time, Sergio has lived in Canastota, and has been employed not only in his hometown, but in Syracuse and Rome as well. By trade Sergio is a cabinetmaker.

In the last decade or so, Sergio has bought a muck farm. This, while working in factories whenever possible, he has operated to the present time. In 1931, he built his own home in the village.

BIBLIOGRAPHY

Davie, Maurice R., *World Immigration*, New York, The Macmillan Co., 1936.

Fairchild, H. P., (Ed.) *Immigrant Backgrounds, The Italians*--Chapter VIII by Bruno Roselli.
New York, John Wiley and Sons, Inc., 1927.

Foerster. R. Franz, *The Italian Emigration of Our Times*, Cambridge, Harvard University Press, 1919.

Hammond, Mrs. L. K., *History of Madison County*, Syracuse, Truair Co., 1872.

Lord, Eliot, and Barrows, *The Italian in America*, New York, B. F. Buck Co., 1905.

Reports of the Immigration Commission. Commission appointed under Congressional
Act of Feb. 1907. Emigration Conditions in Europe, Vol.4.

Smith, James H., History *of Chenango and Madison Counties*, Syracuse, D. Mason & Co., 1880

Smith, John E. (Ed.), A *Descriptive and Biographical Record of Madison County.* New York,
Boston, The Boston History Co., 1899.

Steiner. Edward A., *On the Trail of The Immigrant*, New York, F. H. Revell Co., 1909.

Stephenson, George V., *A History of American Immigration. 1820-1924*, Boston & New York, Ginn and Company, 1926.

Taylor, Paul S., *Mexican Labor in The United States*, Berkeley, University of California Press, 1930.

Villari, Luigi, *Italian Life in Town and Country*, New York and London, G.P. Putnam & Sons, 1910.

Periodicals:

Annual Reports of the Commissioner General of Immigration, United States Department of Labor

The Canastota Bee Journal, Published Weekly by the Canastota. Publishing Co. (In particular, The Golden Anniversary Edition of September 3, 1937.)

1930 Directory of Canastota and Wampsville, Canastota Classified Business Directory compiled and published by the Chamber of Commerce, Canastota. New York. (Material was gathered by a house-to-house canvas).

ENDNOTES

Preface
[1] The United States Census of 1930 reported 49,238 rural farm and 168,138 rural non-farm Italian foreign-born out of a total of 1,792,424
[2] In Central Italy this system was known as the Tuscan Mezzeria

Chapter I Italian Background
[1] Reports of the Immigration Commission, Vol. 4-Chapter III, Passim
[2] Reports of the Immigration Commission, Vol.4-Chapter III
[3] Reports of the Immigration Commission, Vol. 4, Chapter III
[4] Reports of the Immigration Commission, Vol. 4, Chapter III, Passim

Chapter II Italian Immigration to the United States
[1] Davie, M.R., "World Immigration," Page 108
[2] Reports of the Immigration Commission, Vol. 4, Page 138
[3] Reports of the Immigration Commission; Vol. 4, Page 138
[4] Foerster, R.F.: Italian Emigration of Our Times – Pages 323-327
[5] Reports of the Immigration Commission: Vol. 4, Page 138
[6] Reports of the Immigration Commission; Vol. 4, Page 138
[7] Twelfth Census of the United States
[8] Reports of the Immigration Commission; Vol. 4, Page 138
[9] Thirteenth Census of the United States
[10] Idem.
[11] Davie, M.R.: World Immigration, Page 114
[12] Idem.
[13] Primary Source – Commissioner General of Immigration. Quoted from Reports of the Immigration Commission and Davie's "World Immigration."

[14] Fifteenth Census of the United States – 1930, Vol. II
[15] Abstract of Fifteenth Census of the United States – 1930, Page 134
[16] Percentage from 1870-1910 calculated from Thirteenth Census fo the United States; 1910, Vol. I, Pages 800, 834, 835; for 1920 from Fourteenth Census of the United States; 1920, Vol. II, Pages 697-699 and for 1930 from Fifteenth Census of the United States; 1930, Vol. III, Page 53. Quoted from Thompson, W.S., and Whelpton, P.K.: Population Trends in the United States, Page 63

Chapter III Brief History of Canastota
[1] The sources used for this chapter were found in the Canastota Library and in the main were: "A Descriptive and Biographical Record of Madison County," edited by John E. Smith; "The History of Chenango and Madison Counties" by James H. Smith; and "The History of Madison County" by Mrs. L.H. Hammond. The authenticity of these works and the competence of the writers are not known, but they were the best material available. Other references are cited.
[2] Smith, John E.: "A Descriptive and Biographical Record of Madison County."
[3] Idem., Page 274
[4] Smith, J.E.: "A Descriptive and Biographical History of Madison County," Page 276
[5] Tenth Census of the United States
[6] Eleventh Census of the United States
[7] Twelfth Census of the United States
[8] Thirteenth Census of the United States
[9] Idem: Although not all of these were Italians, the majority, as will be shown later, were.
[10] Fourteenth Census of the United States
[11] Idem.
[12] Taken from the Seventh to the Fifteenth Census of the United States – inclusive.

Chapter IV Early Development of the Mucklands
[13] Canastota Bee Journal; Golden Anniversary Edition, September 3, 1937

[1] Sources: The Canastota Been Journal – Golden Anniversary Edition, 1937..Also, information gathered from a number of elderly Canastotans, among whom was John H. Wilson, one of the pioneer muckland owners and one of the community's leading citizens. Other sources are specified.

[2] Judge Barlow's Scrap Book: Vol. IV, Page 174. (Excerpt from the Canastota Herald of November 1868).

[3] Information secured from the Eighth Report of the United States Department of Agricvulture Field Operations, Bureau of Soils, 1906, Page 161.

[4] A commission ditch is one dug under the supervision of a group of men appointed by the State for that particular project. These are the primary drainage ditches.

[5] Canastota Bee Journal – Golden Anniversary Edition, 1937.

[6] Canastota Bee Journal – Golden Anniversary Edition, 1937

[7] Map II

Chapter V The Coming of the Italians to Canastota

[1] This division is arbitrary, and Southern Italy includes the provinces of Calabria, Basilicata, LoPuglie, Compania, and Molise; Central Italy consists of Lazio, Abruzzi, Umbria, Marche, and Tuscany; the remaining Northern provinces make up Northern Italy. The Sicilians, of course, come from the Island of Sicily. Though the information as to section was second hand, the sources were so sound and extraneous checks so that the figures can be accepted as fully authentic.

[2] See prior footnote.

[3] Source: The cases interviewed.

[4] See Table 5.4

[5] See Table 5.5

[6] Source: The cases interviewed.

[7] This, precisely, is the reason given for coming to Canastota, not the occupations after they arrived in the village.

[8] Source: From the cases

[9] Source: From the cases

[10] From the cases

[11] From the cases
[12] Three of these Sicilians were merchants as well as onion growers. A number of others, non-Sicilians, had dual occupations, but the main means of subsistence is considered here.

Chapter VI Italian Ownership of Muckland
[1] Chapter IV
[2] See Table 5.4
[3] Procedure of one of the individuals.
[4] See Map II
[5] This distinction is desired because while in the process of computing the figures from the Tax Records, it was necessary to use the Records of both the towns of Sullivan and Lenox.
[6] The first known Italian operator (on the share system) was James Cordanaro. (Canastota Bee Journal – Golden Anniversary Edition). The first Italian operation occurred around 1897.
[7] These names, years and acreage are derived from the Tax Records of the Towns of Lenox and Sullivan.
[8] Name changed from Bucci.
[9] Source: The Tax Records of the towns of Sullivan and Lenox.
[10] These figures on the total acreage are not exact in all instances, as some difficulty was encountered by the writer in a number of instances where an Italian possessed a farm which included both uplands and mucklands.
[11] This rise in price may be accounted for, among other reasons, by the fact that there is a scarcity of muckland; also because the land, in almost all cases, has been cleared.

Chapter VII The Population of Canastota
[1] In this study, first generation Italians refers to those of foreign birth; second generation Italians are American born children of foreign born Italians or mixed parentage.
[2] Chapter II

[3] This material, with the exception of the figures on the Italian population, was drawn from the Tenth or the Fifteenth Census of the United States, inclusive.
[4] Through the courtesy of Leon Truesdell, Director of the Division of Population in the Bureau of Census at Washington, D.C., a special count was made from the original population schedules. This information is not available in the regular Census.
[5] Estimated by best statistical method possible.
[6] Second generation Italians.
[7] First and second generation Italians.

Chapter VIII The Italians in Agriculture
[1] These small onion bulbs, called "little sets," are usually grown by these same onion growers. They are raised not on muckland but on the uplands, where the hardiness of the grounds does not permit the onions to attain full growth.
[2] These are called "topping" machines.
[3] Information from Charles Farfaglia.
[4] Canastota Bee Journal – Golden Anniversary Edition.
[5] This is not the time nor the place to deal with the question of why labor of women is less in evidence. To determine this would require a special study.
[6] This does not include those Italian-Americans that had permanent residence on the farms.
[7] Other makes have been used but the Dodge, because of its light weight and because it is geared low, is by far the most efficient and satisfactory.
[8] Computed from the Canastota Classified Directory of 1930, with male heads of families as Italian Foreign Born.
[9] Male heads of families being Italian foreign born.
[10] Computed from the Canastota Classified Directory of 1930. With Italian foreign-born as male heads of families.

Chapter IX Italians in Other Occupations
[1] Table 8.1
[2] Source: Computed from Canastota Classified Directory of 1930. Male heads of families being foreign-born.

Appendix
[1] Michael Patterelli, b. 1864, d. 1949.
[2] This is authentic, as Mike produced his citizenship papers for the writer's benefit.
[3] Authentic, as the writer has investigated the Tax Records of the towns of Lenox and Sullivan.
[4] Salvatore D'Amico, b. 1881, d. 1953.
[5] Sergio Grilli, b. 1889, d. 1968.

Made in the USA
Lexington, KY
11 August 2010